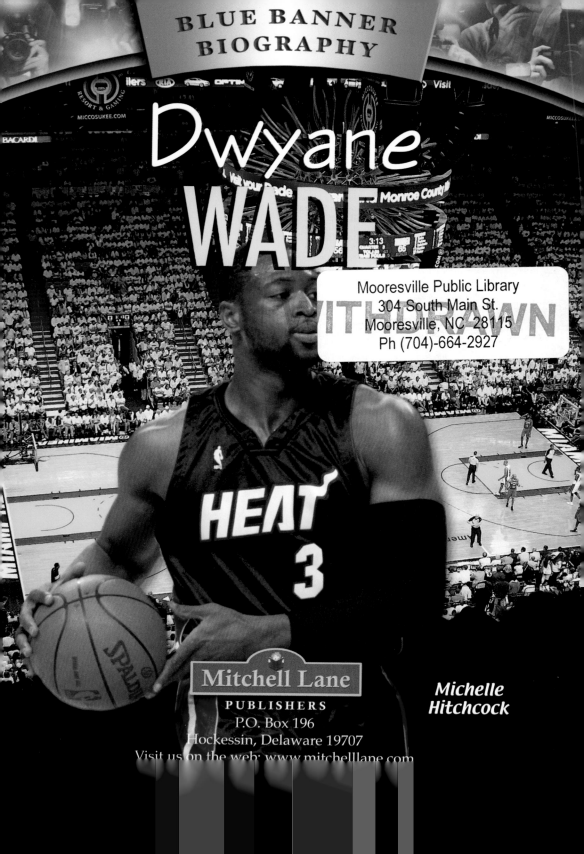

BLUE BANNER
BIOGRAPHY

Dwyane WADE

Mitchell Lane
PUBLISHERS
P.O. Box 196
Hockessin, Delaware 19707
Visit us on the web: www.mitchelllane.com

Michelle
Hitchcock

Mitchell Lane
PUBLISHERS

Printing   1   2   3   4   5   6   7   8   9

Blue Banner Biographies

5 Seconds of Summer	Ice Cube	Miguel Tejada
Abby Wambach	Ja Rule	Mike Trout
Adele	Jamie Foxx	Nancy Pelosi
Alicia Keys	Jason Derulo	Natasha Bedingfield
Allen Iverson	Jay-Z	Nicki Minaj
Ashanti	Jennifer Hudson	One Direction
Ashlee Simpson	Jennifer Lopez	Orianthi
Ashton Kutcher	Jessica Simpson	Orlando Bloom
Avril Lavigne	JJ Watt	P. Diddy
Blake Lively	J. K. Rowling	Peyton Manning
Blake Shelton	Joe Flacco	Pharrell Williams
Bow Wow	John Legend	Pink
Brett Favre	Justin Berfield	Pit Bull
Britney Spears	Justin Timberlake	Prince William
Bruno Mars	Kanye West	Queen Latifah
CC Sabathia	Kate Hudson	Rihanna
Carrie Underwood	Katy Perry	Robert Downey Jr.
Chris Brown	Keith Urban	Robert Pattinson
Chris Daughtry	Kelly Clarkson	Ron Howard
Christina Aguilera	Kenny Chesney	Russell Wilson
Ciara	Ke$ha	Sean Kingston
Clay Aiken	Kevin Durant	Selena
Cole Hamels	Kristen Stewart	Shakira
Condoleezza Rice	Lady Gaga	Shia LaBeouf
Corbin Bleu	Lance Armstrong	Shontelle Layne
Daniel Radcliffe	Leona Lewis	Soulja Boy Tell 'Em
David Ortiz	Lil Wayne	Stephenie Meyer
David Wright	Lionel Messi	Taylor Swift
Derek Jeter	Lindsay Lohan	T.I.
Drew Brees	LL Cool J	Timbaland
Dwyane Wade	Ludacris	Tim McGraw
Eminem	Luke Bryan	Tim Tebow
Eve	Mariah Carey	Toby Keith
Fergie	Mario	Usher
Flo Rida	Mary J. Blige	Vanessa Anne Hudgens
Gwen Stefani	Mary-Kate and Ashley Olsen	Will.i.am
Hope Solo	Megan Fox	Zac Efron

Library of Congress Cataloging-in-Publication Data
Hitchcock, Michelle.
  Dwyane Wade / by Michele Hitchcock.
      pages cm. — (Blue banner biographies)
  Includes webography.
  Includes bibliographical references and index.
  ISBN 978-1-68020-091-1 (library bound)
  1. Wade, Dwyane, 1982– Juvenile literature. 2. Basketball players— United States — Biography— Juvenile literature. 3. Miami Heat (Basketball team)— History— Juvenile literature. I. Title.
  GV884.W23H57 2016
  796.323092 — dc23
  [B]
                                                                    2015017147

eBook ISBN: 978-1-68020-092-8

ABOUT THE AUTHOR: Michelle Hitchcock is a teacher librarian for junior and senior high school students. Her instructional focus is on research and technology. She has played basketball and coached a junior varsity basketball team. Hitchcock lives with her husband and three children on their dairy farm in Upstate New York.

PUBLISHER'S NOTE: The following story has been thoroughly researched and to the best of our knowledge represents a true story. While every possible effort has been made to ensure accuracy, the publisher will not assume liability for damages caused by inaccuracies in the data and makes no warranty on the accuracy of the information contained herein. This story has not been authorized or endorsed by Dwyane Wade.

Blue Banner Biography

NBA player Dwyane Wade (R) and actress Gabrielle Union attend the 2013 ESPY Awards at Nokia Theatre L.A. Live on July 17, 2013 in Los Angeles, California. They married on August 31, 2014.

The Bus Ride

Nine-year-old Dwyane Wade and his fourteen-year-old sister Tragil (Trah-gill) stepped on the bus to go to the movies. Their parents divorced when Wade was a baby and Tragil had always taken care of Dwyane. Their mother Jolinda Morris Wade was addicted to drugs, she was an alcoholic, and she was often not able to care for the children.

As Tragil and Dwyane left the South Side of Chicago where they lived with their mother, Dwyane watched out the window. Their neighborhood was poor and there were drugs and gangs. When their mother forgot to pay the electric bill, they did not have electricity. Other times, they did not have enough food. Once in a while the police raided their apartment to look for drugs, and sometimes the police took their mother away to prison, which scared Dwyane. Tragil usually got him out of the apartment before the police arrived, and they often went to their grandmother's apartment for safety.

As the bus continued down the street, Dwyane saw gang members. He also saw the parks and the basketball courts where kids were playing basketball. Tragil was quiet

Jolinda Wade cut the ribbon to celebrate the opening of the building her son bought for her church in 2008. After she overcame her drug and alcohol addictions and turned her life around, Jolinda became a pastor and started the Temple Praise Church in Chicago.

during the ride. Although Dwyane thought the bus ride was taking a long time, he enjoyed the ride. Tragil always protected him.

Dwyane saw that they were near Bessie McDaniel's (their father's girlfriend) apartment. When he saw Donny, Bessie's son, playing basketball, Tragil and Dwyane decided to get off at that bus stop; the movie could wait. Dwyane liked playing ball with Donny.

Hours later, Tragil asked Dwyane if he was ready to go, but Dwyane wanted to stay. Tragil said Dwyane could stay the night if he wanted, and she would be back the next day. But, Tragil did not come back the next day, or the day after that. By the end of the week Dwyane realized she was not coming back.

When Tragil took Dwyane on that bus ride, she knew they needed help. Dwyane would soon be pulled into the world of gangs and drugs if he stayed in their neighborhood. Their father had to help Dwyane, and Tragil knew it. That bus ride to the movies changed the course of the young boy's life. Even at nine, Dwyane knew Tragil made a tremendous sacrifice when she took him to their father, and he always appreciated that sacrifice. "Still deep down, I understood that Tragil had saved my life."

Wade's World Foundation sponsors basketball camps for youth in Chicago and South Florida. Wade enjoys teaching kids how to improve their basketball skills.

Miami's Dwyane Wade (left) and Shaquille O'Neal celebrate after the team won the 2006 NBA Championship. They played with heart on Coach Pat Riley's "15 Strong" team to win the championship title.

Life Lessons

Dwyane Tyrone Wade, Jr. was born on January 17, 1982 to Jolinda Morris Wade and Dwyane Tyrone Wade, Sr. (Jolinda called Dwyane's father Big Dwyane). Wade's sister Tragil Wade was five years old when Dwyane was born, and Jolinda had two older daughters, Deanna and Keisha, before she married Big Dwyane. Wade's parents divorced shortly after Dwyane was born. Tragil and Dwyane both lived with their mother and occasionally saw their father on weekends.

Willie Mae Morris, Wade's maternal grandmother, is an optimist. She taught Dwyane to focus on the happy memories and he knew he could rely on his grandmother for help.

Life changed for Dwyane after Tragil took him to live with his father. Big Dwyane's girlfriend Bessie McDaniel had two boys, Demetrius and Donny and the three boys often played basketball together. When Dwyane first moved in with his father, the boys had no rules. After the family moved to 69th and Harper streets, things changed. Big Dwyane had served in the Army and he decided to apply some of his military training at home and so he established house rules. When the family moved to Robbins, Illinois, Big Dwyane applied more rules and gave more chores. The young boys did not like that new system, but they knew they had to follow their father's rules.

Big Dwyane and his basketball friends from Chicago put up a basketball hoop for the boys. Basketball games between the boys continued, and through basketball father and son bonded.

Big Dwyane and his basketball friends from Chicago put up a basketball hoop for the boys. Basketball games between the boys continued, and through basketball father and son bonded. The boys attended Harold L. Richards High School in Oak Lawn, Illinois. It was there that Demetrius became a high school basketball star. Between playing ball with his stepbrothers and a growth spurt Wade became a better player. With the help of Coach Jack Fitzgerald and assistant Gary Adams, Dwyane became a star and broke the school basketball records.

While he was in high school, he started dating Siohvaughn Funches. They married while he was at Marquette University. On February 4, 2002, his son Zaire Blessing Dwyane Wade was born, and Dwyane was thrilled. Dwyane and Siohvaughn's marriage was difficult. Five years later, another son, Zion Malachi Aramis Wade was born on May 29 in Chicago. In 2010, Siohvaughn and Wade divorced.

Divorce is difficult for families, and is especially difficult for the children. The Wade's divorce was even more challenging because Dwyane worked for the Miami Heat in Florida and Siohvaughn went back to Chicago to live with the boys. Dwyane traveled to Chicago to see Zaire and Zion, and his sister Tragil brought the boys to Florida to visit Wade. Life was extremely difficult for Dwyane during this time because he missed his boys and he did not like fighting with Siohvaughn so that he could see them. After many problems, Dwyane decided to file a lawsuit to gain full custody of Zaire and Zion, which he later won.

Zaire and Zion's cousin, Dahveon Morris often visited Miami with them before they moved to Florida. Dahveon's mother Deanna Morris is Dwyane's sister. With Deanna's permission, in the fall of 2011 Dahveon moved to Miami to join Wade's family. In Wade's book *A Father First*, Dwyane explained his mission. "Since I'd gotten into the NBA, I had tried to do more for the younger members of our extended family who were living with some of the challenges that I'd experienced when growing up . . . I thought maybe this was my way to 'pay it forward' and step up on [Dahveon's] behalf, as others had for me."

Wade's family continues to grow. His son Xavier Zechariah Wade was born on November 10, 2013. Although Xavier was born out of wedlock with Aja Metoyer, Dwyane is proud to have Xavier as his son. On December 2013, with the help of Zaire and Zion (who made signs that said, "Will you marry us?"), Wade proposed to Gabrielle Union. The couple married August 30, 2014, in Miami and celebrated with family and friends.

In Wade's two years of play at Marquette, he scored 1,281 points and averaged 19.7 points per game.

CHAPTER 3

Coaching Lessons

Many coaches helped Wade become the player he is today. His first coach was his father, and basketball was one of the connections between them. When Dwyane played ball with his stepbrothers as they grew up, Big Dwyane coached them. Big Dwyane also played pick-up games on Sundays. His specialty was playing on the inside and dunking. Dwyane watched his father and the other men play, and he learned from them.

At Harold L. Richards High School in Oak Lawn, Illinois, Coach Jack Fitzgerald taught Dwyane to be a team player. Although Dwyane was the best player on the team, Coach Fitzgerald taught him the importance of being a good team leader. Everyone on the team matters and contributes in some way, and a good leader finds each person's strengths to help the team win.

When Chris Bosh and LeBron James joined the Miami Heat, Dwyane took Coach Fitzgerald's lessons to heart. During a *New York Times* 2011 interview, Dwyane answered a boy's question regarding who was the best player on the Miami Heat team. "It doesn't work without any one of us,"

Wade said. All you can say is, it's Micky Arison's team. He's the owner of the Miami Heat."

Assistant coach Gary Adams taught Dwyane about hard work and determination, encouraging him to work year round if he wanted to play ball after high school.

Adams told Dwyane to learn from other great athletes. In *A Father First*, Dwyane recalls a trip to DePaul University where they watched Quentin Richardson play. Adams pointed out Richardson's style, "Look at that, see the dribble, you can do that." Dwyane understood that Adams "wanted to show me things that others did well and that I could choose to add to my own game." Dwyane set school records for both steals (106) and points (676).

After high school, Head Coach Tom Crean at Marquette University was the person who helped Dwyane. Crean gave him a chance to improve his grades so that he could play basketball at the college level. Although Dwyane was not eligible to play during his first year, Crean used that time to develop Wade's skills. Coach Crean encouraged Dwyane to observe his teammates, analyze what they did right, and figure out how they could fix what they did wrong. While Dwyane memorized statistics and thought about how to coach his teammates, he realized that he could apply those same skills of recall analysis to his studies so that he could overcome his test anxiety. It worked. Dwyane's grades improved and

> *Coach Tom Crean at Marquette University gave him a chance to improve his grades so that he could play basketball at the college level.*

he was eligible to play basketball with Marquette University's Golden Eagles the next season.

At Marquette University, after the first year of ineligibility, Dwyane played for two years. In his two years of play, he scored 1,281 points and averaged 19.7 points per game. He helped his team all the way to the National Collegiate Athletic Association (NCAA) Tournament's Final Four in 2003. His success during his junior year at college brought him to the attention of professional basketball team scouts.

Coach Crean believed in Dwyane. During the semifinals of the Midwest Region against the second seeded (a position in a playoff or tournament) Pittsburgh Panthers, Marquette's Golden Eagles played badly in the first half of the game. In *A Father First* Wade remembered what Crean told him at half-time, "Dwyane, listen, if this is going to be your last game, just go put it on the line." Dwyane did put it on the line and pushed himself to play better than he thought possible. The Golden Eagles had a terrific second half and won the game, and Dwyane proved he was ready to play in the National Basketball Association (NBA).

Coach Pat Riley coached the Miami Heat "15 Strong" during the NBA 2005-2006 season. Every member of the team mattered, making the team "15 Strong." But, after a crushing loss by thirty-six points in the regular season to the Dallas Mavericks, Riley wanted to know if the Heat had the heart to play the game. At the end of the season, the Heat played the Mavericks for the NBA Championship title. The Heat lost the first two games in the series, and then Riley's team of "15 Strong" played with heart to win the next four games and the championship.

Germany couldn't stop Wade (#9) and the rest of Team USA in the 2008 Olympics in China. Team USA defeated Spain to win the gold medal and earned the nickname the Redeem Team.

CHAPTER 4

Taking the Heat

When Dwyane was married to Siohvaughn Funches and he had Zaire, his one-year-old son, he had to consider his family as well as his career. He chose to leave college before his final year to play professional basketball. The Miami Heat chose Dwyane Wade in the fifth round of the June 2003 NBA draft. By the end of his first season with the Heat, he was selected for the NBA All-Rookie First Team. He went on to play in the 2004 United States Olympic team, which won the bronze medal.

The 2005-2006 season brought highs and lows. The season started off with too many losses. Heading into the postseason, teammate Shaquille O'Neal's injuries limited his time on the court, which affected his statistics. Dwyane recalls Shaq's response, "Stats don't matter. I care about winning, not stats. If I score zero points and we win, I'm happy." Shaq's views on the team and winning impressed and influenced Dwyane. Under Coach Pat Riley, the "15 Strong" Miami Heat team won its first NBA championship in 2006 against the Dallas Mavericks. Dwyane won the Finals' Most Valuable Player award for his basketball and leadership skills averaging 34.7 points and 7.8 rebounds per game.

In 2008 Dwyane again played for Team USA along with LeBron James and Chris Bosh. Although the three men knew each other, the three teammates became better friends playing together at the Olympics, and they wondered what it would be like to play on the same NBA team, especially after Team USA won the gold medal and earned the nickname the Redeem Team.

> **When the fans watched Dwyane play ball they did not know all the issues he had at home. Behind the scenes, Dwyane was in the middle of an intense custody battle for his children.**

Dwyane became a free agent in 2010. Miami wanted him to stay with the Heat and they launched the We Want Wade Campaign to convince Wade to stay. He did stay and his former Olympic teammates Chris Bosh and LeBron James joined him. The season started off slowly, but they improved. When the fans watched Dwyane play ball they did not know all the issues he had at home. Behind the scenes, Dwyane was in the middle of an intense custody battle for his children.

On March 11, 2011, Dwyane won full custody of his boys, Zaire and Zion. The next day, the Heat played the Memphis Grizzlies. Dwyane's enthusiasm about his boys showed in his game. With twenty-eight points, five rebounds, nine assists, three steals, and five blocks, he significantly contributed to the 118 to 85 win over the Grizzlies. The *ESPN* headline read, "Dwyane Wade Turns Back Grizzlies as Heat Turn up D in Romp." The Heat continued to the NBA finals, but they lost to the Mavericks in six games with both Wade and James earning places on the NBA All-Star team.

The team's momentum for success was set in motion. But, in June 2011 the NBA owners started a lockout, which cancelled pre-season games as well as regular season games with the season not starting until Christmas Day. The short season was still successful for the Heat as they took the title for the Eastern Conference, but Dwyane suffered from knee problems that affected his play during the conference games and he required surgery after the finals. As they headed into the 2012 Finals, after losing the first game, the Heat, with LeBron James leading the way, came back to win the next four games and take their second championship title.

Dwyane Wade (far left) celebrates with his Miami Heat teammates after they win game seven against the San Antonio Spurs to capture the 2013 NBA Championship Title at the American Airlines Arena on June 20, 2013 in Miami, Florida.

Miami Heat guard Dwyane Wade (R) shoots as San Antonio Spurs guard Danny Green (L) defends in the first half of their NBA Finals game five at the AT&T Center on June 15, 2014 in San Antonio, Texas.

The Heat continued its winning pattern the following season. Again they won the Eastern Conference Title. Those NBA Championship Finals are considered among the best in the league's history. The Heat was matched against the San Antonio Spurs. The Spurs were up by one game when they entered the sixth game. The Spurs led by three points with twenty seconds remaining. LeBron James shot a three pointer but missed. Chris Bosh grabbed the rebound and sent it to Ray Allen who shot from the corner and hit the three point shot. The crowd went wild as the game went into overtime. The Heat won game six in an overtime battle 103-100. They also took game seven for a consecutive championship title.

For Dwyane and the Heat, wins and losses are all part of the game and the season.

The 2013-2014 season ended with another Eastern Conference title; however, after the humiliating loss to the Heat in game six of the 2013 Finals, the Spurs rallied to dominate the 2014 Finals winning in five games. For Dwyane and the Heat, wins and losses are all part of the game and the season. Focusing on their accomplishments of four consecutive years winning the NBA Eastern Conference Title (2011-2014) and three NBA titles (2006, 2012, and 2013) helps motivate the team even when they take second place. The Heat fell short of the Eastern Conference title in 2014-2015. In 2015, Wade became a free-agent. The Miami Heat still wanted him on their team, and Wade agreed to a twenty million dollar contract for the 2015-2016 season.

Dwyane Wade reads with Davard Johnson and Makayla Refuse of Liberty City Elementary during Wade's World Foundation '3 Under the Tree' holiday event at the Miami Children's Museum on December 18, 2014.

Wade's World

*I*n his book *A Father First*, Dwyane remembered his first prayer, "If you take me and my sister out of this place and you save our mother, I will be someone worthy of your help and I'll be the best dad and take care of my family when I grow up, and I'll be good to other people, too; and if I jump out of line or make a mistake, I'll admit it and get back on the right road."

In 2003, after starting in the NBA, Dwyane established Wade's World Foundation (WWF) to promote health, literacy, and fatherhood. In 2007, his sister Tragil Wade became the executive director of the foundation. Under her direction, the foundation and its programs have grown. WWF focuses its support in Chicago where Wade grew up, Milwaukee where he attended college, and Miami where he lives and works. As part of its global outreach, WWF does help other communities in need.

Wade's mother, Jolinda Wade overcame her drug and alcohol addictions, turned her life around, and became a pastor. In Chicago WWF worked with Pastor Jolinda Wade and New Creation Binding and Loosing Ministries

International to establish the Live to Dream program. Through their collaboration The Live to Dream program sponsored a free six-week summer program for children ages eight to fourteen with summer reading instruction in 2012 and 2013.

In Miami, WWF also sponsors a Live to Dream program. From this, the foundation developed the Live to Dream Challenge, a new program for the young people who live in the Miami area. The WWF website explains the new Live to Dream Challenge, "The community-focused program was developed to inspire young people to 'do good' in their communities." Young people create community service projects and complete them. When the group completes three projects, they receive tickets to a Miami Heat home game.

In December 2014, the WWF *Facebook* page announced another Live to Dream program in Milwaukee. The summer reading program is for second and third grade students in inner-city Milwaukee neighborhoods. The foundation works with Marquette University to help promote literacy to children. To help start the program, people attending the December 6 Marquette men's basketball game against Wisconsin donated 1,332 books.

The Reading Takes You Far campaign started in June 2012 in Chicago with Wade, the Chicago Public Library, and the children of By The Hand Club. The campaign gave free books to children in Chicago. With Wade's support, they also created the "Text To Donate" program so people can donate money to help buy more books. Books encourage reading and promote literacy and Dwyane knows, "The better you can read, the faster you can learn, and the more successful you can be in life."

WWF and the Sandals Foundation sponsors The Game Changer program. The two foundations work together to help poor children in South Florida and the Caribbean. Game Changer provides coaches and mentors for youth. By December 2014 they had repaired eleven sports courts and provided sports equipment to the youth to play games.

WWF also sponsors three-day basketball camps. Boys and girls ages eight to sixteen in Chicago and South Florida are eligible for this opportunity. The basketball camps teach the boys and girls about basketball, life-skills, hard work, and teamwork. WWF and Dwyane Wade make certain that basketball and life lessons are both valuable components of the camp. Wade helps with the camps, as do the Women's National Basketball Association (WNBA) and NBA players; Alonzo Mourning, Quentin Richardson, and Tyrus Thomas have all helped.

Beyond Chicago, Miami, and Milwaukee, WWF has helped other communities in need. When Hurricane Katrina hit New Orleans, Louisiana, Dwyane Wade personally delivered survival kits to homes in need and WWF helped rebuild three homes there. WWF has donated money to schools and organizations in other parts of the United States to help repair or build new basketball courts. Helping communities who help young people is yet another example of how WWF gives back to the community.

Dwyane Wade's world reaches far beyond his family and friends. He remembers those people who helped him in the past and he offers financial support to organizations that provide programs to help young people. Basketball was an outlet for Dwyane and he sees athletics as an opportunity for youth to be physically fit and learn the team concept. That bus ride with Tragil to live with his father gave Dwyane the chance to do more with his life. Wade's NBA basketball success became the opportunity for him to provide support to his family and to help others while being "a father first."

1982	Dwyane Wade is born on January 17, in Chicago, Illinois. His parents Dwyane Wade, Sr. and Jolinda Morris Wade divorce.
1992	Dwyane Wade and his family moved to Robbins, Illinois.
2002	Dwyane Wade marries Siohvaughn Funches. Son Zaire Blessing Dwyane Wade is born on February 4 in Miami, Florida.
2003	The Marquette University Golden Eagles go to the NCAA Final Four basketball tournament. In the winning game against Kentucky, Wade has a triple double (twenty-nine points, eleven rebounds, and eleven assists). Wade is named an All-American. In June, he is selected by the Miami Heat in round five of the NBA draft. He establishes Wade's World Foundation.
2004	Wade is a member of the USA Olympic team that won the bronze medal.
2006	The Miami Heat wins the NBA Championship. Wade wins the NBA Finals Most Valuable Player (MVP) Award for averaging 34.7 points, 7.8 rebounds, and 3.8 assists.
2007	Zion Malachi Aramis Wade is born on May 29, 2007 in Chicago, Illinois. Tragil Wade is named the executive director of Wade's World Foundation.
2008	Wade is a member of the USA Olympic team that wins the gold medal.
2010	Dwyane and Siohvaughn Wade divorce. Wade decides to stay with the Miami Heat and signs a contract for fourteen million dollars for the season. Wade wins the NBA All-Star MVP Award.
2011	Dwyane Wade is granted full custody of his children on March 11. The Miami Heat wins the Eastern Conference Title.
2012	The Miami Heat wins the Eastern Conference Title and the NBA Championship. Wade releases his book *A Father First.*
2013	The Miami Heat wins the Eastern Conference Title and the NBA Championship. Xavier Zechariah Wade is born on November 10 in Los Angeles, California.
2014	The Miami Heat wins the Eastern Conference Title. The Heat takes second place to the San Antonio Spurs in the NBA Championship Games. Gabrielle Union and Dwyane Wade are married on August 31.
2015	Wade opts out of his contract and becomes a free agent. Wade returns to the Miami Heat and signs a contract for twenty million dollars for one-year.

Year	Team	FGM	3PM	FTM	REB	AST	BLK	STL	TO	PTS
'03-'04	MIA	371	16	233	247	275	34	86	196	991
'04-'05	MIA	630	13	581	397	520	82	121	321	1,854
'05-'06	MIA	699	13	629	430	503	58	146	268	2,040
'06-'07	MIA	472	21	432	239	384	62	107	216	1,397
'07-'08	MIA	439	22	354	214	354	37	87	224	1,254
'08-'09	MIA	854	88	590	398	589	106	173	272	2,386
'09-'10	MIA	719	73	534	373	501	82	142	252	2,045
'10-'11	MIA	692	63	494	485	346	87	111	237	1,941
'11-'12	MIA	416	15	235	237	225	63	82	129	1,082
'12-'13	MIA	569	17	308	344	352	56	128	194	1,463
'13-'14	MIA	415	9	189	241	252	29	79	161	1,028
'14-'15	MIA	509	29	284	219	299	21	73	209	1,331
Career		**6,785**	**379**	**4,863**	**3,824**	**4,600**	**717**	**1,335**	**2,679**	**18,812**

(FGM- Field goals made, 3PM- Three-pointers made, FTM- Free throws made, REB- Rebounds, AST- Assists, BLK- Blocks, STL- Steals, TO- Turnovers, PTS- Points)

2004 Unanimous NBA All-Rookie First Team
USA Olympic Team Member (Bronze)
2005 NBA All-Star Game
2006 NBA Championship Title with the Miami Heat
NBA Finals MVP
NBA All-Star Game
Sports Illustrated Sportsman of the Year
Sports Illustrated for Kids Athlete of the Year
2007 NBA All-Star Game
2008 USA Olympic Team Member (Gold)
NBA All-Star Game
2009 NBA All-Star Game
2010 NBA All-Star Game
NBA All-Star MVP Award
2011 NBA All-Star Game
2012 NBA Championship Title with the Miami Heat
NBA All-Star Game
2013 NBA Championship Title with the Miami Heat
NBA All-Star Game
2014 NBA All-Star Game
2015 NBA All-Star Game

Books

Wade, Dwyane. "Dwyane Wade: My Life as an NBA Single Dad." *Newsweek*. June 6, 2011. http://www.newsweek.com/dwyane-wade-my-life-nba-single-dad-67923

Wade, Dwyane with Mim Eichler Rivas. *A Father First: How My Life Became Bigger Than Basketball*. New York: William Morrow, 2012.

Works Consulted

Abrams, Jonathan. "Wade's Busy Weekend Gives Him Time to Relax." *The New York Times*. February 22, 2011. http://www.nytimes.com/2011/02/22/sports/basketball/22wade.html?_r=0

"All Time League Leaders." *NBA.com/Stats*. December 30, 2014. http://stats.nba.com/leaders/alltime

Associated Press. "Dwyane Wade Turns Back Grizzlies as Heat Turn Up D in Romp." *ESPN NBA*. March 12, 2011. http://scores.espn.go.com/nba/recap/_/id/310312014/gameId/310312014/memphis-grizzlies-vs-miami-heat

"Dwyane Wade." *Facebook*. December 30, 2014. https://www.facebook.com/dwyanewade

"Dwyane Wade." *NBA*. December 30, 2014. http://www.nba.com/playerfile/dwyane_wade/

"Dwyane Wade" *Marquette Men's Basketball*. http://www.gomarquette.com/sports/m-baskbl/mtt/wade_dwyane02.html

Goodman, Joseph, Dwyane Wade. "Miami Heat Reach One-Year $20 Million Deal." Miami Herald. last modified July 2, 2015. http://www.miamiherald.com/sports/nba/miami-heat/article26134327.html

Kumar, Sujay. "My Favorite Mistake: Dwyane Wade." *Newsweek*. October 15, 2012. http://www.newsweek.com/ dwyane-wade-phone-call-changed-his-life-65481

Miami Heat's Dwyane Wade Makes Gift to Marquette University to Enhance Literacy for Inner-City Children. *Marquette University News Center*. December 1, 2014. http://news.marquette.edu/news-releases/ dwyane-wade-gift/

"My Story." *Dwyane Wade*. December 29, 2014. http://dwyanewade.com/about/my-story/

"NBA Season Recaps." *NBA History*. NBA Media Ventures. July 1, 2014. http://www.nba.com/history/nba-season-recaps/index.html

"Overview." *Wade's World Foundation*. 2014. http://www.wadesworldfoundation.org/about-us/ overview/

"Programs." *Wade's World Foundation*. 2014. http://www.wadesworldfoundation.org/programs/ overview/

"Reading Takes You Far." *Wade's World Foundation*. December 29, 2014. http://www.readingtakesyoufar.com/ aboutus/

"Season Review: 2011-2012." *NBA History*. *NBA Media Ventures*. March 4, 2013. http://www.nba.com/history/ seasonreviews/2011-12/index.html

"Season Review: 2012-2013." *NBA History*. *NBA Media Ventures*. June 19, 2014. http://www.nba.com/history/ season-review-2012-13/index.html

Stengel, Richard. "10 Questions for Dwyane Wade." *Time*. September 24, 2012. http://www.time.com/time/ magazine/article/0,9171,2124409,00.html

Wade, Dwyane. "Dwyane Wade: My Life as an NBA Single Dad." *Newsweek*. June 6, 2011. http://www.newsweek.com/dwyane-wade-my-life-nba-single-dad-67923

Wade, Dwyane with Mim Eichler Rivas. *A Father First: How My Life Became Bigger Than Basketball*. New York: William Morrow, 2012.

"Wade Signs Reported Two-Year Deal with Heat." *NBA. NBA Media Ventures*. July 15, 2014. http://www.nba.com/2014/news/07/15/heat-resign-wade.ap/

"Wade's World Foundation." *Facebook*. https://www.facebook.com/WadesWorldFoundation

On the Internet

"All Time League Leaders." *NBA*. http://stats.nba.com/leaders/alltime

Dwyane Wade http://dwyanewade.com/

"Dwyane Wade." *Facebook*. https://www.facebook.com/dwyanewade

"Dwyane Wade." *NBA*. http://www.nba.com/playerfile/dwyane_wade/

"NBA Season Recaps." *NBA History*. http://www.nba.com/history/nba-season-recaps/index.html

Wade's World Foundation http://www.wadesworldfoundation.org/

"Wade's World Foundation." *Facebook*. https://www.facebook.com/WadesWorldFoundation

INDEX